MW01519461

High Crimes and Low IQs

50 of the Dumbest Criminals

ABSOLUTE CRIME

By William Webb

Absolute Crime Books

www.absolutecrime.com

Table of Contents

3

Introduction

Dumb criminals don't just make the jobs of police officers around the world easier, they also make for great entertainment. The exploits of stupid bandits, dimwitted thieves, and bungling burglars make for great reading and titillating television.

Best of all, there is an unending stream of such dimwits in all corners of the world. The internet and YouTube now ensure that the antics of dumb criminals will be seen and enjoyed by millions of web surfers. Many others will be entertained by reading about such boneheads and it is easy to see why.

The sheer stupidity of dumb criminals is unbelievable and entertaining in itself. Many of these criminals' stories are not just entertaining, their exploits are almost too incredible to believe, yet they are all true. So laugh your heads off and don't get scared because most of these stupid crooks are only a threat to themselves.

Aaron Smith

You would think that a corrupt cop could become a highly effective criminal. Aaron Smith proved that stupid cops can become very dumb criminals because he was arrested for stealing from police headquarters.

That's right; he thought he could get away with stealing stuff right out of the police station under the nose of his comrades. Smith even broke into a lockbox and stole cash from the police department. The whole affair was even more embarrassing because Smith was a seven-year veteran of the Tempe, Ariz., police department.

Smith apparently thought that nobody would notice that a lockbox had been broken into and $750 in cash removed. He also believed that nobody would notice that two police bicycles were missing.

Incredibly, he apparently stole the items during his shifts at the police station.

If that wasn't bad enough, at least one of the items that he stole didn't even work. It was a GPS unit that was broken, so he pitched it in the garbage.

It didn't take the world's best internal officer to catch Smith. A detective who suspected him caught him by handing him a purse full of money to check in as evidence. When Smith didn't turn the purse in, the detective knew who was stealing from the police station.

Then, to prove how stupid he was, guess where Smith stored the stuff he stole from the police station? He stored the bicycles and other loot at his own house. Detectives found it there when they served a search warrant and searched the residence.

Aaron Smith's crime spree was so petty that he only earned 90 days in the county jail. The total value of his loot came to less than $1,000. That's right; Smith committed petty theft and threw away his career in the process.

There's no word on what Smith will do once he gets out of jail. One thing's obvious; he doesn't have much of a future as either a criminal or a cop.

Bibliography

Associated Press "Ex-Tempe police officer Aaron Smith sentenced in theft case." 7 June 2013. abc15.com. Wire Service News Article. 12 June 2013.

Hendley, Matthew. "Aaron Smith, Ex-Tempe Cop, Gets 90 Days in Jail for Being a Petty Thief." 7 June 2013. blogs.phoenixnewtimes.com. News Blog Entry. 11 June 2013.

—. "Aaron Smith, Ex-Tempe Cop Pleads Guilty to Stealing from Police Department." 12 April 2013. blogs.phoenixnewtimes.com. News Blog Entry. 12 June 2013.

Alan Golden

Some criminals have to be blind as well as stupid, as Alan Golden proved when he tried to avoid paying for his dinner. Golden thought he could get away with a "dine and dash" by eating a meal in a restaurant and then running off before the check came at an Applebee's in Las Cruces, N.M. on March 1, 2012.

There was only one problem. The restaurant was hosting a "Tip-A-Cop" event, a charity fundraiser in which uniformed police take the place of the regular wait staff. Any tips the officers collected were given to a local charity. That's right, he tried to commit a crime in a restaurant full of uniformed police officers.

If that wasn't dumb enough, he didn't notice the fact that the waiters and waitresses were police officers! The person that Golden was trying to cheat out of a tip was a police officer. Golden figured that he could get up and simply walk out the door without paying for his $30 dinner.

When Golden got up and tried to flee, police grabbed him and placed him under arrest. He ended up in the county jail on a charge of stealing services less than $100.

Perhaps it's a good idea to take a look around at your surroundings before you try to break the law. You really should notice things like the presence of a large number of police officers.

Golden not only cheated Applebee's, he also cheated the New Mexico Special Olympics, which was the beneficiary of the event. In other words, he basically stole from a charity in full view of the police.

What's worse is that Golden might have been on some sort of date when he tried to skip out on his meal tab. News reports indicate that he was eating dinner with two women before he tried to walk out without paying. Getting arrested for not paying the dinner check is not a good way to impress a woman.

Bibliography

Lohr, David. "Alan Golden, 'Dine and Dash' Suspect, Arrested During Police Fundraiser." 5 March 2012. huffingtopost.com. Huffington Post News Feature. 13 June 2013.

Albert Bailey

Some people obviously expect a higher level of customer service than others. One very stupid criminal, Albert Bailey of Fairfield, Conn., expected a ludicrous level of customer service from his local bank.

On March 23, 2013, Bailey called a People's United Bank branch in Fairfield and made a very unusual request. He asked bank employees to put all the cash in the facility in a bag and sit it out for him to make his robbery easier. That's right, he called ahead and told his victims when he was coming to rob them.

Not surprisingly, the victims called the police, but they also complied with Bailey's wishes. They put $900 in cash in a money bag and sat it out for the crooks to pick up. About 10 minutes later, Bailey drove up in a car and sent an unidentified accomplice into the building to retrieve the loot. The accomplice wasn't identified because he was under 16 and it would be illegal for police to release his name to the media.

When the accomplice came out of the bank and handed the loot to Bailey, police moved in and placed the two dimwits under arrest. The bank did give excellent customer service – it complied with Bailey's request.

Helping the Police Make the Case

The bank also gave police the evidence they needed to arrest and charge Bailey for robbery. Thanks to his phone call, police were there to witness the accomplice leaving the bank with the money and handing it to Bailey. They were able to catch the two morons red handed.

Planning ahead can help criminals get away with a crime, but some plans such as Bailey's seem to be a means of getting to jail faster. One has to wonder what was going through Bailey's mind when he made that call. Didn't he think that bank employees might call the police?

Good customer service apparently does pays off for People's United Bank. Its employees were able to help police nail two of the stupidest bank robbers in the world.

Bibliography

Associated Press "Police: Robbers called Conn. bank for money to go." 24 March 2013. boston.com Wire Service News Article. 9 June 2013.

Amritpal Mehat

Pretending to be dumb is actually a very dumb defense. At least that's what a not-so-bright embezzler from Manchester, England named Amritpal Mehat discovered.

When Mehat was arrested for stealing £408,000 ($633,394) from various post office box store franchises in 2009, he came up with an incredibly stupid defense. He told prosecutors and police that God had made him dumb and mute as a punishment for his crimes. That meant he could no longer speak, but he apparently could.

Okay, Mehat was pretty dumb. He thought that nobody would notice that $633,394 was missing. He also thought that he could cover his tracks by using one of his employees' computer user names. That ruse failed when that employee quit working for Mehat's business, but he kept using the user name to cover his theft, even after investigators audited his books and discovered what was going on.

"God Made Me Dumb" Defense

The "God made me dumb" defense didn't work either. Neither the jury nor Judge Bernard Level believed Mehat's claim, and Mehat was sentenced to four years in prison. Insulting the intelligence of the jury and blaspheming the Almighty is obviously not the way to win the sympathy of the court.

If that wasn't bad enough, Mehat didn't realize that the court might send him to a mental hospital for evaluation by trained psychologists. That's exactly what happened, and the experts discovered that Mehat was not dumb at all.

In fact, the mental health experts discovered that Mehat speaks at least two languages, English and Punjabi (an Indian dialect). Mehat actually began talking to a psychologist at a mental hospital that he was sent to by prison authorities.

He had claimed he could no longer speak because of God's punishment, yet he was able to speak in two different languages. One also has to wonder if Mehat was going to call God to court to testify on his behalf.

Judge Level actually said Mehat was "mute by malice" when he sentenced the nitwit. All Mehat proved was that he was even dumber than anybody had suspected.

Bibliography

PTI "Indian-origin conman turns dumb to avoid UK jail." 13 July 2012.
articles.timesofindia.indiatimes.com Wire Service News Article. 10 June 2013.

Arron and Rhianna Thomas

Contrary to popular belief, embezzlers are often among the dumbest criminals. Many of them make little or no effort to cover up their thefts. Take the case of Arron and Rhianna Thomas from Oxfordshire, England.

Arron Thomas stole over £100,000 ($156,000) from the company where he was working and made absolutely no attempt to hide it. Arron Thomas simply wrote a series of fake invoices with his fiancée's name on them and had the company make out checks that he began depositing into her bank account.

Some of the purchases included breast implant surgery for Rhianna, a new car, a new Suzuki motorcycle, and more. The two even held a lavish wedding on the same day as Prince William and Kate

Middleton. They celebrated their wedding by going on a shopping spree with cash they didn't own.

Police Work Made Easy

Not surprisingly, it wasn't long before observers noted that the Thomas's were living large on Arron's salary as a ledger (accounts payable) clerk. The theft was made worse by the fact that Thomas had just taken the job. The thefts began right after he went to work; it wouldn't take the most brilliant police officer to suspect him.

Arron Thomas's past criminal record, which included jail time for fraud, made him an even better suspect. The fact that the money was going straight to Rhianna Thomas's bank account didn't help her case.

Arron Thomas was sentenced to 22 months in prison, while Rhianna had her 15-month prison sentence suspended because the judge found she was under his "spell." That probably wasn't the home, nor the honeymoon the newlyweds wanted.

They proved that living a life of luxury while earning a working class salary is not a good way to cover up the crime of embezzlement, nor is depositing the funds in your bank account under your name. White collared crimes can be just as dumb and as easy to catch as street hoodlums.

Bibliography

Robson, Steve. "Newlywed jailed for £100,000 fraud as his wife is spared prison for spending the money on breast surgery, a motorbike and a new car." 1 May 2013. dailymail.co.uk. Daily Mail Feature Article. 11 June 2013.

Ata Yousef El Ammouri

Some criminals just never seem to learn as the case of former Chicago storekeeper Ata Yousef El Ammouri reveals. El Ammouri knew that there was a murder warrant out for him in Chicago, yet he returned to the Windy City after a 33 year absence.

The Chicago Tribune reported that sheriff's deputies were waiting for El Ammouri at O'Hare International Airport when he stepped off a plane on June 7, 2013. El Ammouri apparently thought he could return to Illinois from Jordan where he had been living because nobody would remember him after all these years.

The law apparently has a very long memory, but Mr. El Ammouri obviously does not. He forgot that there is no statute of limitations on murder. A person can be tried for murder decades after the crime.

The reason El Ammouri returned to the US was apparently to attend a graduation of some sort. Returning to face arrest is bad enough, but returning to listen to a long-winded speech and eat a cake shaped like a graduation cap is even worse. Couldn't El Ammouri's relatives have simply taped the graduation and let him watch it on YouTube?

Murder for Beer

What's even dumber is the motive for the murder El Ammouri is alleged to have committed back in 1979. He shot a man named Joe Harris who allegedly stole a can of beer from a convenience store El Ammouri had been running on Chicago's South Side.

El Ammouri killed a man, threw away the American dream, wrecked his business, and ruined his own life over a can of beer. After Harris's shooting, El Ammouri was arrested and jailed but released on a $100,000 bail. He skipped town and fled to Jordan.

El Ammouri will never get to see the graduation he returned to attend because he's locked up in jail. Instead, he'll have to watch the whole thing on

YouTube on the jail computer. Obviously some criminals don't get any smarter with age.

Bibliography

Chicago Tribune Staff "Fugitive in 1979 Chicago slaying arrested at O'Hare." 8 June 2013. chicagotribune.com Newspaper Article. 8 June 2013.

Big Scores Don't Make Smart Robbers

Some robbers don't get away with big heists because of their own incompetence. Simply increasing the amount of money that you're trying to steal does not increase the intelligence of the crooks.

There was the gang of armored car robbers near Kuala Lumpur, Malaysia, that had to leave most of the cash behind after a September 2008 holdup. The bandits had to leave the loot behind because their getaway car wasn't big enough to haul the money. Cops told reporters that the crooks left nine bags containing the equivalent of $786,000 in the armored car.

It doesn't pay to use an economy car as your getaway vehicle. Planning obviously wasn't that gang's strong suit. If they had simply brought a van, they could have been able to haul the cash away.

Blowing up the Bank

The Malaysian bandits were geniuses compared to a pair of robbers in Dinant, Belgium. The two tried to blast open a bank's ATM machine in an attempt to help themselves to some free cash.

The problem was that they used too many explosives and set it off too quickly. The explosion destroyed the bank and killed both of the robbers. The robbers were trapped when the bank collapsed.

Police think the crooks tried to pump some sort of explosive gas into the bank and for good measure set off several sticks of dynamite. The crooks not only used too many explosives, they didn't have the good sense to get away before setting off the explosion.

The criminals may not have known how to use the explosives when they blew the bank. It pays to be careful when you're blowing a safe or an ATM. The explosion wasn't the subtlest method of robbery either; it woke up everybody in town, including the police.

The two criminals did win a sort of award posthumously; the Darwin Award, which is given to those who do the most to improve the human race by leaving it. The Award's presenters evidently thought those two qualified.

Bibliography

Agencies "Armed robbers forced to leave cash because getaway car too small." 30 September 2008. telegraph.co.uk. Wire Service News Article. 11 June 2013.

Alleyne, Richard. "You were only supposed to blow the bloody doors off!!" 2 January 2010. telegraph.co.uk. Daily Telegraph Column. 11 June 2013.

Mail Foreign Service. "Two bank robbers are killed by their own explosives after trying to blow up bank safe." 28 September 2009. dailymail.co.uk. Wire Service News Article. 11 June 2013.

Charles and Pernella Bull

The two dumbest burglars in America are Charles and Pernella Bull of South St. Paul, Minn. Not only did they commit one of the stupidest burglaries of recent years, but they also gave the dumbest excuse for a crime possible. The couple tried to claim that an imaginary Craigslist ad gave them the right to pillage somebody else's home.

The Bulls simply walked into a home on May 17, 2011 and started removing items, including a laptop computer. They didn't even check to see if anybody was in the home, even though the homeowner and her kids were in the house.

When the woman heard somebody moving around, she came downstairs and saw the Bulls running out the backdoor with her stuff. The two put the stolen goods on their bicycles in full view of a witness and started to ride off, but they didn't get very far because a neighbor blocked their getaway with his car.

Craigslist Gives us the Right to Loot Homes

The police arrived shortly afterwards and took the Bulls into custody. The couple didn't help their case by telling officers a fantastic story. They claimed they saw the woman's home listed on Craigslist as a free house that owners had to vacate immediately. They said that gave them the right to enter the home and steal the woman's possessions.

The police didn't believe the Bulls' story, which became less credible when an officer checked Craigslist and found no such ad. The story was apparently a bald-faced lie.

Mrs. Bull also claimed that she thought the house was vacant, yet she found such items as a laptop, a desktop computer, and the woman's purse in the home. They also found a full tool kit. These

30

possessions were found in Charles Bull's duffle bag by the police.

The Bulls now face criminal charges that could earn each of them a 20-year prison sentence and $35,000 in fines. The moral of the story is that there is no such thing as a free house.

Bibliography

WCCO "Couple Charged with Burglarizing South St. Paul Home." 27 May 2011. minnesota.cbslocal.com. News Story. 12 June 2013.

Charles Rodriguez

Even dumb criminals can sometimes steal a lot of money as the case of Charles Rodriguez of Manchester, England, proves. In 2011 Rodriguez was able to get away with stealing more than $100,000 worth of jewels and successfully fled England.

Rodriguez and another gang member ambushed a jeweler in Manchester and stole the diamonds. They then skipped to South America by using fake passports.

Rodriguez would have gotten away with the crime if he hadn't posted pictures of himself on his Facebook page. Instead of lying low, the dimwitted bandit put pictures of his vacation and a shopping trip to London online. It was the London trip that led to Rodriguez's arrest.

The robber probably thought he was safe because he had returned to his homeland of Colombia, which does not have an extradition treaty with the United Kingdom. Yet he made the mistake of returning to Britain on a fake passport in December 2012, when he was still wanted. To make matters worse, he posted pictures of himself in a place where British police could arrest him online while he was still in England.

Police saw the Facebook pictures and started looking for Rodriguez in London. They did not have to look very long because constables pulled Rodriguez over on a traffic stop. He gave them the fake passport but forgot about the fact that police could check his fingerprints; they did and arrested him.

Charles Rodriguez won't be returning to Colombia for some time. Instead, he'll spend the next five years in one of Her Majesty's prisons because of his own stupidity.

If he had just stayed out of England, Rodriguez would have been able to remain free and spend his loot. He might have even able to stay free in London and return home if he had not posted his vacation photos on Facebook.

Once again Facebook has helped a less than brilliant criminal get himself caught. Perhaps the police of the world should give Mark Zuckerberg a special award for creating Facebook; he made their job a lot easier. Facebook gives police an easy means of locating dumb criminals.

Bibliography

Dolak, Kevin. "Thief Busted After Posting Vacation Pics." 15 January 2013. news.yahoo.com. ABC News Blog. 19 July 2013.

Claud Gipson-Reynolds

Some criminals compound a crime with one dumb move after another. One of the worst was a California man named Claud Gipson-Reynolds. In 2004, Gipson-Reynolds made the news by stealing a fire truck.

Gipson-Reynolds made the dumb criminal hall of fame by what he did with the truck. First, he drove out of the fire station without opening the door, doing thousands of dollars in damage. Then he got the fire truck stuck in the mud and finally, he used the truck's radio to call for help.

Gipson-Reynolds committed the crime after getting drunk and having a fight with his wife. He drove off into a remote rural area in Napa County in his car. When his car got stuck, Gipson-Reynolds went looking for help.

Fire Truck Theft

The only structure in the area was a small firehouse operated by the local volunteer fire department. Gipson-Reynolds broke in but couldn't find a phone. He did find a small fire truck and decided to use it to pull his car out of the mud.

Gipson-Reynolds didn't even open the firehouse door; he drove straight through it. Then he went to retrieve his car. But instead of retrieving it, he got the fire truck stuck in the mud, too.

Gipson-Reynolds then realized that he could use the fire truck radio to call for a tow truck. He called 911 and explained what had happened. The 911 operators didn't send a tow truck; they sent the California Highway Patrol, which placed Gipson-Reynolds under arrest. After committing breaking and entering and grand theft auto and doing thousands of dollars' worth of damage to the firehouse, Gipson-Reynolds called the police and told them where he was.

36

World's Dumbest Criminals

Even Gipson-Reynolds admitted how stupid his crime was. He later told a reporter: "I could probably get on that show, *World's Dumbest Criminals*." He also admitted: "I was pretty intoxicated at the time. My thinking was not the best."

A judge released Gipson-Reynolds on bail after he promised to start attending Alcoholics Anonymous. Among other crimes, Gipson-Reynolds was charged with drunk driving and grand theft auto.

Bibliography

Fox News "Grand Theft Fire Truck." 8 November 2004. foxnews.com. Fox News Feature Article. 7 June 2013.

Colin Small

There are effective ways to dispose of evidence, and then there's the way that Colin Small disposed of evidence. The Virginia political operative simply threw at least eight voter registration forms into a dumpster in full view of witnesses.

To make matters worse, Small threw the forms into the wrong dumpster. He pitched them into a container that was only used for cardboard. Rob Johnson, the manager of a Tuesday Morning thrift store in Harrisonburg, Va., saw Small pitch the forms while taking a smoke break. When he examined the papers, Johnson realized that they were voter registration forms.

It was against the law for Small, who was working for a contractor to the Republican Party, to simply throw the forms away, because they contained Social

Security numbers. Under the law, he was supposed to destroy the forms or face felony charges.

Small was arrested in October 2012, right before the Presidential election, after Johnson went to the police. He was first charged with a felony that was later reduced to a misdemeanor.

Too Lazy to Use a Paper Shredder

Basically, Small was arrested because he was too lazy to use a paper shredder. He also obviously didn't know how to read, because cardboard only dumpsters are clearly marked as such. Some of them are even painted a different color to make it easy to recognize them.

It isn't known why Small was throwing the forms out, although one of them contained the name of a convicted felon, who was ineligible to vote. He may have been trying to dispose of evidence of voter fraud. If that's the case, he didn't do a very good job of it.

The case against Small led to criminal charges and generated nationwide headlines. He clearly didn't do a good job of covering up his criminal activities. Obviously, political operatives thinking of committing voter fraud shouldn't hire Colin Small nor should they follow his lead and throw evidence in the wrong dumpster.

Bibliography

Reilly, Ryan J. "Witness 'Disgusted' Felony Charges Dropped Against Colin Small in GOP Voter Registration Case." 3 April 2013. huffingtonpost.com. Huffington Post News Feature. 11 June 2013.

Tanfani, Joseph "Virginia Judge dismisses voter fraud felony charges." 2 April 2013. latimes.com. LA Times News Blog. 11 June 2013.

David Weber

The popular news website, the Huffington Post, labeled David Weber as one of America's stupidest criminals, and it is easy to see why. He used a stolen credit card to try to pay for beer at a bar in Miami Beach in September 2011.

There was only one problem; the credit card that Weber tried to use to buy the beer belonged to the bartender. The bartender was completely dumbfounded when he saw his own name on the credit card that he had just been handed. The victim apparently filled Weber's order even though he was paying for it.

Weber got the credit card from a car in the bar's parking lot. He broke into the car sitting outside the bar and didn't think that the car's owner might just be inside the bar.

After he recovered his wits from the shock of being handed his own credit card, the bartender called the police. The police came and arrested Weber at the bar.

Weber, who claimed to be homeless, said he had found the credit card lying on the ground. Police didn't believe his story and booked him into the Miami-Dade County Jail on credit card and theft charges.

The beer that Weber ordered turned out to be a very expensive one. Interestingly enough, the news articles don't say whether Weber actually got his beer or not. They simply state that he was arrested after trying to pay for the beer.

The moral of the story is clear; if you steal credit cards, at least take them someplace else. It's also clear that laziness can land a criminal in jail just as quickly as stupidity. Had David Weber been willing to walk down the street to another bar, he might have gotten away with his crime.

At least Weber got a place to sleep for the night out of the deal, although not one he may have wanted. Perhaps he should try paying for his own beer next time.

Bibliography

Associated Press "David Weber, Miami Beach Man, Tried to Buy Beer with Bartender's Own Stolen Credit Card." 12 September 2012. huffingtonpost.com. Wire Service News Article. 7 June 2013.

Smiley, David. "Miami Beach police: Man tries to buy beer with card stolen from the bartender." 11 September 2012. miamiherald.com. Miami Herald Newspaper Article. 7 June 2013.

Donald Gartner

Donald Gartner of Port Richey, Fla., found the worst possible place to break into cars: the jailhouse parking lot. Gartner was actually caught trying to break into cars right after he was released from jail. He didn't even wait until he got off of jail property to start committing crimes.

To make matters worse, there was apparently a woman inside the first car he tried to break into. The woman started screaming, which didn't deter Gartner. He started trying to break into another car in full view of a police officer, who had just dropped another crook off at the Pasco County Jail.

The officer went and got the deputies from inside the jail. The deputies arrested Gartner and took him right back in.

Attacking a Porch Light

Attempted car theft wasn't the first stupid crime Gartner had committed on the night of Oct. 2, 2011. Earlier in the night Gartner had reportedly attacked his neighbor's porch light. He shook the light so hard that its panels fell out.

The upset neighbor called sheriff's deputies, who found a drunken Gartner crawling around in the bushes at his neighbors' house. The deputies took Gartner to jail, where he made bail around 10 p.m. Instead of going home, Gartner tried to break into cars.

Reports indicate that Gartner told deputies he thought one of the vehicles was his car that he could use to drive home in. That proves just how dumb or drunk Gartner was. His car was back at his house because the deputies presumably hauled him to jail in a patrol car.

If you want to break into cars, the jailhouse parking lot isn't a good place to do it. It's also a good idea to be sober when you commit crimes. At least Gartner spared the taxpayers the cost of a ride to jail; he was already there.

Bibliography

Huffington Post. "Donald Gartner Arrested in Jail Parking Lot Hours After Being Released." 4 October 2011. huffingtonpost.com. Huffington Post Weird News Feature. 10 June 2013.

Lonon, Sheri. "Attempted Auto Burglary at Jail Results in Arrest." 3 October 2011. landolakes.patch.com/articles. Land O'Lakes Patch Newspaper Article. 10 June 2013.

Erin James

Some criminals keep doing the same things over and over again. A classic example is a Chicago-area woman named Erin James.

Police in Riverside Ill., a Chicago suburb, pulled James' car over and arrested her for drunk driving on May 4, 2013. The crime was a dumb one because James was driving home from a celebration at a local bar.

What was the celebration? She had been holding a drinking party to celebrate the return of her driver's license. The license was suspended last year because James had been arrested for drunk driving.

James even told the officer who pulled her over why she had been celebrating. Not surprisingly, the officer tested her breath and found it over the legal limit.

Interestingly enough, James was pulled over in the same town, possibly by the same cops for the same crime. James was also speeding at the time of her arrest, giving police a reason to pull her over.

So James is not going to be getting her license back anytime soon. She might lose her driving privileges completely this time. A judge had earlier ordered her to only drive vehicles that contain something called the breath alcohol ignition interlock device. That's an electronic gadget that stops a car from starting if you have too much alcohol on your breath. The officers who pulled James over noted that she didn't have such a device on the car she was driving.

The moral of this story is a simple one: the next time you hold a party for the return of your license after a drunk-driving suspension, take a taxicab home. That way, you won't have to hold another celebration next year. At least Erin James has a reason to celebrate next year. If she's smart, she'll take a cab home from that party.

Bibliography

Chicago Tribune Staff "Police: DUI charge for woman celebrating end of earlier DUI suspension." 4 May 2013. chicagotribune.com. Newspaper Article. 8 June 2013.

Frankie Portee

If you plan to try and fool the police with a false identity, choose one that doesn't happen to belong to a wanted criminal. That method of evading capture didn't work so well for Frankie Portee of Springfield, Mass.

Actually, Portee seemed to have done everything in his power to get himself arrested. He was riding in a car with an expired inspection sticker and not wearing a seatbelt. In other words, he gave state troopers two good reasons to pull over the vehicle, which they did.

When the cops approached the car, Portee gave them the false name of Daniel Atkins, but there was only one problem. There was an arrest warrant out for Daniel Atkins, and Atkins looked similar to Portee.

When State Trooper John Driscoll checked the

police computer, he found the warrant and decided to arrest Portee.

Portee got up and ran over to a nearby Starbucks, where two other state troopers were enjoying their coffee. His short getaway ended in the back of the police car with handcuffs.

It was later learned that Portee used the fake name because he was wanted for violating probation. He was also found to be in illegal possession of a firearm.

The fake ID incident occurred in 2010, and Portee is still in state prison in Massachusetts. Recent news reports indicate that he tried to appeal his conviction for resisting arrest. Strangely enough, a judge upheld his conviction.

If he had chosen a good fake ID or simply worn his seatbelt, Frankie Portee might have gotten away with the crime. Worst of all, Frankie Portee wasn't even driving the car when it was pulled over. Two unidentified women were driving the vehicle.

Note to criminals: it pays to check and see who's wanted in your area. That way, you won't be arrested for somebody else's crime.

Bibliography

Ring, Dan. "Conviction of Frankie Portee of Springfield, who gave false name when cited for not wearing seat belt; upheld by Appeals Court." 28 November 2012. masslive.com. Republican Newspaper Article. 12 June 2013.

Gabriel Gonzalez and Jeremy Lovitt

Criminals need to be careful not to leave their keys in the car just like everybody else. Lame-brained robbers Gabriel Gonzalez and Jeremy Lovitt learned this the hard way at a Burger King in Stockton, Calif. in May 2013.

The two young men went into the burger joint about nine at night with guns drawn. The criminals managed to get the cash and get out of the restaurant. Then they ran into a minor problem: the getaway car was gone.

The two had left the getaway car running and unattended with the keys in it. The car was also unlocked to make a would-be thief's job easier.

While Lovitt and Gonzalez were forcing the Burger King employees to open the safe and the cash registers, another employee ran outside. That employee saw their car sitting there, jumped in and drove off, leaving the two dimwits stranded at Burger King.

Fortunately, the two didn't have to wait long for a ride. The robbers tried to get away by running across a field but they were unable to outrun a police car. Officers found guns and the stolen cash on the two robbers. Lovitt and Gonzalez, both 19, got a ride to jail.

The getaway car was still in the area. The brave or cowardly employee had simply driven it around the block. News reports didn't say whether the employee who drove away in the vehicle would be charged or not.

The lesson from this story is an obvious one. Never leave the getaway car, unlocked, running, unattended, and with the keys in it. It might not be there when you need it, when the robbery is over. One has to wonder how Lovitt and Gonzalez are going to be able to face their fellow criminals when they reach prison.

Bibliography

Huffington Post. "Jeremy Lovitt, Gabriel Gonzalez, Robbery Suspects, Stranded When Burger Employee Takes Getaway Car." 24 May 2013. huffingtonpost.com. Huffington Post News Feature. 9 June 2013.

James, Paul. "What happens when a robbery victim steals the crooks' getaway car?" 24 May 2013. news10.net. News Article. 9 June 2013.

VanOlson, Cora. "Smart Employee Steals Dumb Robbers' Getaway Car." 28 May 2013. trutv.com/library/crime/blog. Blog Entry. 9 June 2013.

Gabriel Perez-Majia

Hiding in the clothes dryer isn't a very good way to avoid arrest. That's what dim-witted burglar Gabriel Perez-Majia discovered when he was captured in a house in New Rochelle, N.Y., a New York City suburb.

Perez-Majia broke into the home of Aaron and Gwen Stone on June 13, 2013, but he obviously wasn't a very effective prowler. The bungler tripped a burglar alarm almost as soon as he entered the home. This brought the police, who noticed a broken window.

Perez-Majia looked outside and noted that the house was completely surrounded; he had no way to get away. So what did he do; give up and enjoy a nice ride in a police car? No, he went back inside and hid.

Left a Trail for Police to Follow

The criminal mastermind apparently thought that he could evade the law by hiding in the clothes dryer. Yet he neglected one minor detail: a trail of blood leading straight to the dryer.

When Perez-Majia refused to give up, officers came inside and they brought a police dog named Tank. They really didn't need Tank's help, because a trail of blood led straight from a pile of loot to the clothes dryer.

Perez-Majia got arrested and became eligible for additional charges, such as evading arrest. In other words, his attempt to evade the law in the clothes dryer will earn him more prison time.

One also has to wonder how long Perez-Majia intended to stay in the dryer. Was he going to be in there for several hours until the police left? That wouldn't be very comfortable or very healthy. He also didn't seem to realize that police would search the house and bring a police dog.

Hopefully prison authorities in New York have a good sense of humor and put Perez-Majia to work in the prison laundry. He seems to like laundry facilities; perhaps he'll enjoy working in one.

Bibliography

Journal News Staff. "New Rochelle K-9 nabs burglary suspect in dryer." 12 June 2013. lohud.com. Journal News Newspaper Article. 14 June 2013.

Krumboltz, Mike. "Police catch alleged burglar hiding in clothes dryer." 13 June 2013. news.yahoo.com. Yahoo News Blog. 14 June 2013.

Houaka Yang

No criminal might be dumber than Houaka Yang. The Wisconsin resident used a stolen camcorder to record a video of himself. Yang was even polite enough to identify himself on the video to make it easier for police to find him.

Yang stole the camera from Chris Rochester, a local Republican Party operative in La Crosse, Wis., in early 2013. The camera was later recovered by police who didn't realize that Yang had used the device to videotape a confession.

When cops returned the camcorder to Rochester, he discovered several videos that Yang had shot with it. One of the videos contained the confession and also showed his home.

But it's Ok the cop won't figure it out

To help police, Yang even said, "This is my house, yes, and a stolen camera that I stole. But it's okay, the cops won't figure it out." Then to make sure police had enough to lock him up, Yang also said, "Oh yeah, to introduce you, my name is Houaka Yang. So yeah, how do you do?"

In case police needed a mug shot, Yang even turned the camera on himself and said, "And this is me. Hi."

That's right; Yang recorded his own confession and left it where somebody could find it. To add to the embarrassment, Rochester posted the video on YouTube so everybody on the web could see what an idiot Yang was. He even titled it "Confessions of a stupid criminal: thief is sure he won't get caught."

News reports noted that this wasn't the first time a video and stupidity led to Yang's arrest. He and another criminal were caught on surveillance video stealing from cars in the driveway of a local politician. Cops were able to track down Yang by showing the video around town.

Largely because of his video performance, Yang now faces charges that carry a maximum sentence of two years in jail and a $30,000 fine. The lesson here is an obvious one – stupid criminals should stay away from recording devices, especially stolen ones.

Bibliography

Ramde, Dinesh. "Houaka Yang, Suspected Thief, Confessed and Identified Himself on Tape with Stolen Camcorder." 23 May 2012. huffingtonpost.com. Associated Press News Article. 6 June 2013.

Houston Gunmen

Breaking into a house and terrorizing the residents isn't a very smart thing to do, especially when you're dealing with an armed resident, as a trio of Houston-area bandits recently found out.

In mid-May 2013 the three kicked in the door of a home on Braeburn Valley Drive in Houston. They easily attacked and overpowered the man inside the house then shoved him into the closet and locked him in so they could ransack the home.

The unidentified bandits made two really dumb mistakes; first they didn't tie up or restrain victim so he couldn't get loose, and second they didn't look to see what was in the closet. The closet was where the owner kept his guns.

Robber Gets Shot

The man picked up his gun, loaded it, and came out of the closet looking for the gunmen. He found them and engaged in a brief shootout in which the bandit was hit by a bullet. When police arrived, they found the hapless robber lying on the street outside the house, bleeding.

The other two criminals were able to make an escape in their SUV. The dimwits left their injured buddy behind, probably not realizing that he would rat them out.

The dumb robber got himself shot, but he also missed some valuable items that are easy to fence on the street. Namely, the homeowner's guns, which could easily be sold on the black market.

The morons also set themselves up for more prison time because armed robbery is a more serious felony than simple burglary. It's also a great way to get shot if something goes wrong, as the bandits found out.

Bibliography

Farberov, Snejana. "'Dumb house burglar shot after locking homeowner inside his own GUN CLOSET." 16 May 2013. dailymail.co.uk. Daily Mail Feature Article. 11 June 2013.

Stanton, Robert. "Intruder shot in gunfire with Houston resident." 14 May 2013. chron.com. Houston Chronicle Article. 11 June 2013.

Jacob Cox-Brown

Some criminals make the job of the police far too easy. A classic example was Jacob Cox-Brown, an 18-year-old from Astoria, Ore. Cox-Brown would have gotten away with drunk driving and hitting two cars if he hadn't posted about it on Facebook.

After a New Year's Eve drinking spree, Cox-Brown drove home and hit two parked cars on the way. When he got home, the first thing Cox-Brown posted was: Drivin drunk...classic;] but to whoever's vehicle I hit I am sorry, :P"

To make the officers' job easier, the Facebook page contained a picture of Cox-Brown, as well as the post, so police would have no trouble finding him. The Facebook tipsters also gave the police Cox-Brown's address.

Drinking and Facebook Don't Mix

Two people who saw this post sent Facebook messages to the Astoria Police Department the next day. The officers who got the message went to Cox-Brown's house and found that his car matched one that they had received complaints about.

Cox-Brown was arrested on two charges of not reporting an accident. Police couldn't charge him with drunk driving because he had already slept off the effects of his New Year's binge.

We've long known that drinking and driving don't mix and can lead to accidents. Jacob Cox-Brown has proved that drinking and Facebook don't mix either.

His arrest shows why it is definitely a good idea for criminals and drinkers to stay away from Facebook. Everybody, it seems, is on the Social Network these days, including the police. Getting yourself caught is easier than ever, thanks to today's technology. You don't even have to leave home to tip off the police.

Strangely enough, Cox-Brown is only one of many criminals who have been captured because they bragged about their exploits on social media.

Bibliography

Bindley, Katherine. "Jacob Cox-Brown, Oregon Teen, Posts Facebook Status About Drunk Driving, Gets Arrested." 4 January 2013. huffingtonpost.com. Huffington Post News Feature. 7 June 2013.

KGW.com Staff. "DUI

 Facebook post lands Astoria teen in jail." 4 January 2013. kgw.com. News Article. 7 June 2013.

James O'Hare and David Dalaia

Some criminals go to a great deal of trouble to commit a stupid crime for very little money. Take Manhattan residents James O'Hare and David Dalaia. They went to incredible lengths to commit small time check fraud.

In 2008 James O'Hare discovered that his roommate Virgilio Cintron had died. Right after he discovered the body, O'Hare found Cintron's $385 Social Security check in the mail. He decided to cash it but he didn't look like Cintron. Instead, he asked Dalaia to help him.

The two dressed Cintron's body, sat it in on an office chair then pushed it down the street to the Pay-O-Matic check cashing store. The morons attracted a large crowd because the body kept slumping over and falling off the chair.

That's right, they tried to push a corpse down a busy New York street on an office chair and believed that nobody would notice. They also expected the check-cashing store employees not to notice that their customer was dead!

They attracted a lot of attention, including NYPD Detective Travis Rapp, who was eating lunch at a restaurant. Rapp looked out the window and saw the two and realized that they were pushing a body.

68

Rapp quickly called 911 and reported what was happening.

Police stopped the two as they entered the door of the check-cashing store. The two were arrested and Cintron's body was taken to the morgue where it belonged. Dalaia and O'Hare found themselves charged with check fraud. Apparently corpses don't make an effective prop for crime.

Worst of all, Cintron was supposedly their friend. If that's how they treat a friend, we'd hate to see what they'd do with an enemy's body.

Bibliography

Hays, Tom. "A Corpse, A Check a Bizarre NYC Crime." 8 January 2008. huffingtonpost.com. Associated Press News Article. 11 June 2013.

pysih.com. "David J. Dalaia and James O'Hare." n.d. pysih.com. Blog Entry. 11 June 2013.

James Phillips

England's dumbest criminal in recent years, James Phillips, chose the worst possible getaway vehicle possible, a moped (or motorized bicycle) with a top speed of around 30 miles per hour. Phillips tried to outrun police cars with a top speed of 150 mph and a police helicopter that moved at 180 mph.

News reports don't indicate why police were chasing Phillips; most likely, they were trying to catch him because he was riding a motorized vehicle through the streets of Bristol without insurance or a license early in February. Phillips' lawyer said his client was simply scared of the police.

It seems a court took Phillips' license away for an earlier dangerous driving incident. During that crime, Phillips was caught driving the getaway car in a burglary. This time, he didn't have a car.

Thinking Skills Needed

The used moped that Phillips was riding had a 50cc engine that was about the same as the engine on a chainsaw or a lawnmower. Press reports indicate the vehicle has a top speed of 30 mph, but Phillips was only moving at 15 mph. Phillips was moving so slowly that a pedestrian nearly punched him off the motorcycle. He also reportedly slowed down for speed bumps, probably because he would have been knocked off by hitting one.

To make matters worse, he drove the bicycle into traffic and in front of cars as police followed him. There was little chance of an effective getaway because a police helicopter was hovering overhead and keeping track of the moron's movements.

A judge at the Bristol Crown Court gave Phillips a suspended sentence and ordered him to perform 100 hours of unpaid community service. The judge also ordered Phillips to enter a thinking skills program – he obviously needs one.

It'll be a while before Phillips is back behind the wheel – he cannot legally drive again for three years. If police catch him driving, he'll have to serve nine months in jail.

Bibliography

Salkeld, Luke. "Four police cars and a helicopter to chase man on a 15 mph moped: The not so nail-biting pursuit where rider even slowed for speed bumps." 27 February 2013. dailymail.co.uk. Daily Mail Feature Article. 10 June 2013.

James Roberts

Social media and crime don't mix – at least that's the lesson Manhattan mugger James Roberts learned the hard way. Roberts was sentenced to five years in prison because he made things easy for police.

72

After mugging a victim and stealing a watch on 10th Avenue in Chelsea, Roberts went home and posted a picture of himself on MySpace.com. In the picture, Roberts was wearing the watch and ring that he had just stolen from his victim. Roberts wanted to show his gang friends his latest trophy.

Roberts' homeboys were not the only ones visiting his MySpace page. Another visitor was a detective from the Manhattan North Gang Intelligence Unit. The detective noticed the expensive jewelry and showed it to the mugging victim. The victim identified Roberts and the stolen goods from the picture.

This enabled police to make a case against Roberts and his cohort in crime, Darryl Calier. The evidence they left on MySpace enabled prosecutors to convict them of mugging.

Interestingly enough, Roberts is not the only dumb crook caught by the Gang Intelligence Unit's use of social media. *The New York Post* reported that the

Unit was able to make a case against heroin dealer "Handsome Rell" Blue in 2010.

Handsome Rell posted a picture of himself on his MySpace page with a wad of cash, and even bragged that he was making $250,000 a year from drug dealing. The information on the MySpace post led police straight to Blue and to charges of selling narcotics.

It just doesn't pay to talk about criminal activity on social media, especially in New York City. Detectives in the Big Apple now routinely check social media to see what gang members and other criminals are chatting about. Some of the gangs make it even easier for cops to monitor their activities by having their own Facebook and MySpace pages. Modern technology makes it easier than ever for technologically savvy cops to track down stupid criminals.

Bibliography

Hamilton, Brad. "Braggarts at 'site' of the crime." 21
November 2010. nypost.com. New York Post Feature
Article. 7 June 2013.

Jeffrey M. McMullen

Jeffrey M. McMullen of North Cambria, Pa. deserves the title of America's dumbest robber. He tried to rob a local bank for just $1 in October 2012, and he had a hard time getting away with it. The tellers actually refused to believe what was happening and wouldn't cooperate.

What was even dumber was McMullen's motive – he wanted to be sent to federal prison. Bank robbery is a federal crime, and the dimwitted McMullen actually believed that he would be sent to the federal prison in Loretto near his hometown.

If all that wasn't stupid enough, McMullen robbed his neighborhood bank, where everybody knew what he looked like. He didn't wear a mask, and the tellers apparently knew who he was. McMullen was actually a regular customer at the bank.

To make matters worse, McMullen wrote the bank robbery note demanding cash in front of tellers and other witnesses so that they could see what he was doing.

$1.00 Bank Robbery

The note said: "Federal bank robbery. Please hand over $1.00. FBI custody. Preferably (sic) Loretto Pa. No press. Seal all files." McMullen obviously didn't realize that the FBI does not take suspects into custody – it hands over those it arrests to other law enforcement agencies for safekeeping. He also expected a federal judge to grant his wishes.

After writing the note, he handed it to the teller, who thought the whole affair was a joke and told him to go the next window. McMullen walked to the next window where he asked for the bank manager and the police.

He was eventually approached by a new accounts employee, who gave him $1 from her purse. Bank employees also complied with his wishes and called the police, who came and took him into custody.

There's no word on whether McMullen got his wishes of being turned over to the FBI or sent to the federal prison in Loretto. Instead, he was indicted on three charges of robbery and held on $50,000 bond. Not surprisingly, a federal judge ordered McMullen, who though he could tell the federal court what to do, to undergo a mental health evaluation.

Bibliography

Reabuck, Sandra K. "Police: Bank robbery note sought $1." 8 October 2012. tribune-democrat.com. Tribune-Democrat Newspaper Article. 7 June 2013.

Jeffrey Dahmer

America's most notorious cannibal and serial killer, Jeffrey Dahmer, belongs on the list of world's dumbest criminals for an obvious reason: he took photographs of his victims' corpses then left them out for the police to find. Dahmer actually created evidence of his crimes and left it out in plain sight to make the investigators' job easier.

Unlike most murderers, who go to great to great lengths to hide their crimes, Dahmer made the homicide detectives' job as easy as possible. When he murdered his victims, mutilated their corpses, and ate their flesh, he took pictures. He left the pictures around his apartment so he could use them as a masturbation aid. If that wasn't enough help for the police, Dahmer also stored several heads of his victims in the refrigerator and penises he had cut off of victims in jars in his house.

The only step Dahmer didn't take was to mail the photos to the police so they could come and visit him. The miracle around Dahmer's killing spree in Milwaukee in the late 1980s and early 1990s was how long it went on. Dahmer did almost everything he could to help police locate him.

On at least two occasions his victims actually broke loose and flagged down police cars. Unfortunately, officers actually brought one of the victims, a Laotian immigrant boy, back to Dahmer's apartment.

Police located Dahmer's apartment on July 22, 1991, when officers found a young man named Tracy Edwards wandering around the streets wearing handcuffs. Edwards told the cops that he had been taken to an apartment, restrained, drugged, and terrorized by a "weird dude."

Intrigued, the officers went to Dahmer's apartment; the first things they noticed were the pictures of his victims lying out in plain sight. Dahmer was quickly arrested and the apartment searched. Police had no problem gathering enough evidence to get Dahmer convicted of murder. The cannibal was killed under suspicious circumstances shortly into his 957-year sentence.

Bibliography

Biography.com. "Jeffrey Dahmer." n.d. biography.com. Biography.com Feature Story. 25 May 2013.

Jonathan G. Parker

Facebook addiction and crime don't mix, at least that's what Jonathan G. Parker of Fort Loudon, Pa. discovered. When he broke into a house in Martinsburg, W.V. to rob it, Parker couldn't stop himself from using the home computer to check his Facebook page.

After chatting with his Facebook friends, Parker left the Facebook page up on the victim's computer. That's right, he left a digital image that showed his name and picture up for police to see. Before he left the house, Parker also helped himself to two diamond rings.

After seeing Parker's name and picture, the victim asked around the neighborhood and learned where Parker was staying. She told the local sheriff's department, which went right out and arrested Parker.

During the search for Parker, the deputies encountered a friend of his who indicated Parker was even stupider than we thought. The friend told the deputies that Parker asked him if he wanted to help him break into the home. The friend said no and told deputies where to find Parker.

Thanks to the Facebook post, Parker ended up in jail facing a 10-year prison sentence and $10,000 in bail for daylight burglary. That was one of the costliest visits to Facebook in history.

If you're planning on a career of burglary, it would make sense to use your own computer to check your Facebook page, or at least log off it when you are done. Had Parker simply logged off, the victim and the sheriff wouldn't have known his identity and had such an easy time finding him.

Facebook is obviously a very good friend to police around the world. Over the past few years, it has helped the law capture scores of extremely stupid criminals. It seems to attract them like honey draws bees.

Bibliography

Dybwad, Barb. "BUSTED: Burglar Arrested After Checking Facebook During Robbery." 17 September 2009. mashable.com. Blog Entry. 12 June 2013.

Marshall, Edward. "Burglar leaves his Facebook page on victim's computer." 16 September 2009. jounal-news.net. Journal Newspaper Article. 12 June 2013.

Krystian Bala

Authors are often advised to base their writings on personal experiences or their own lives. This isn't good advice for murderers and other criminals as Polish author and sadistic killer Krystian Bala found out.

In 2000 Bala tortured and murdered a man named Dariusz Janiszewski and got away with it. Even though police found Janiszewski's body, they didn't have any suspects until Bala published a novel called *Amok.* In the novel, a young woman is tied and bound in exactly the same way that Janiszewski was tied and bound.

Bala described the crime in writing and published it in a book. The book even became a bestseller in Poland. After detectives read it, they took a look at Bala and discovered that he wasn't much of a master criminal.

Bala had a good motive for murdering Dariusz Janiszewski; the businessman had been having an affair with Bala's wife. Bala also took Janiszewski's cell phone and sold it on eBay through an account registered to his name. Before selling the phone, Bala made a number of calls on it to his girlfriend and his parents. He left an obvious trail that police traced right to him.

Though he is a crime writer, Bala is obviously no criminal genius. Even the plot of *Amok* taunted the police; the book portrays police officers as numbskulls that cannot catch murderers. Bala went out of his way to make the police mad at him and show them he was a suspect.

Krystian Bala's career as a murderer was short lived, but he now has plenty of time to write. He was convicted of murder and sentenced to 25 years in prison in 2007. It isn't known if Bala is planning a book on his experiences in prison yet or not. He might also write a book on how to get caught for murderers.

Bibliography

Purvis, Andrew. "Polish Murder Stranger Than Fiction." 6 September 2007. time.com/time/world Time Magazine Feature Article. 13 June 2013.

Marquis Diggs

There are some things that you should never bring to court with you. Illegal drugs are definitely among them, as Marquis Diggs of Jersey City, N.J., found out. The small-time drug dealer arrived at a court hearing on Dec. 17, 2012 with 32 bags of marijuana in his pockets.

Police found the bags on Diggs when they arrested him for an outstanding warrant for another crime. Diggs came to court, even though he knew that he was wanted on charges of dealing drugs within 1,000 feet of a school.

He didn't realize that police might check the court docket, see his name there, and be waiting for him. Nor did he realize that he might run into police officers that might know what he looked like and that there was a warrant out for him at the courthouse.

The saddest part of the affair is that Diggs is very familiar with the court system. Press reports indicate that he has been arrested on drug charges many times before.

Even His Mother Doesn't Like Him

Worst of all was the reason why Diggs was at the Hudson County Administration Building in Jersey City. He was there to protest a restraining order that his own mother had filed against him. Apparently Diggs is such a pest that not even his mother wants him around.

One good thing about the incident is that Diggs' mother may not need to go ahead with the restraining order for a while. He'll be in jail for some time after bringing drugs to court. News reports indicate that Diggs will now face at least three more years of parole for his actions.

Diggs did save the taxpayers of Jersey City some money. Police didn't have to drive out and pick him up. He came to them and committed another crime in front of a pretty impeachable witness: the judge.

Bibliography

Conte, Michelangelo. "Cops: Jersey City man of 32 bags of marijuana in Hudson family court." 17 December 2012. nj.com. Jersey Journal Newspaper Article. 10 June 2013.

Peters, Justin. "Dumb Criminal of the Week: The Guy who brought 32 bags of weed into a courtroom." 27 December 2012. slate.com. Slate Magazine News Feature. 10 June 2013.

Michael Ruse

Nothing seems to destroy dumb criminals faster than Facebook. The stupidest criminal on Facebook was probably Michael Ruse of Leigh Park, England. When he was on trial for assault at the Portsmouth Crown Court, Ruse helped the prosecution with his Facebook posts.

The posts included such statements as "yeah, I think I get away with it." The genius couldn't even spell, nor could he refrain from insulting the judge with the statement "nearly time to leave for crown and see the stuck up judge!"

The genius didn't realize that prosecutors could see what he was posting on Facebook, nor did he think that they would print the posts out and pass them out to the jury. Well, that's exactly what the prosecutors did.

When he was faced with the evidence, Ruse promptly pleaded guilty. He obviously didn't get away with it. Instead, he used Facebook to frame himself.

Ruse and a buddy named Terry Reeve were on trial for a particularly loathsome crime. They had attacked Reeve's father with a baseball bat and a baton. Ruse denied the charge to the jury, but not to his friends on Facebook.

One of the friends wasn't so friendly – he or she told the prosecutors about Ruse's posts. Ruse might have thought he was getting away with it because he was using his alias of "Michael Miles" on Facebook. There was only one problem: Michael Miles' Facebook profile contains a picture of Michael Ruse!

The court gave Ruse a 46-week suspended jail term and sentenced him to house arrest when he wasn't working. The judge clearly wasn't amused by Ruse's antics on Facebook.

"Your stupidity really is not much mitigation," Judge Ian Pearson pointed out to Ruse at his sentencing. Nor was Ruse's barrister or attorney very impressed by his client.

"He needs help with his thinking skills," Russell Pyne told the court. Actually, Michael Ruse needs to learn how to think in the first place.

Bibliography

Ellicott, Claire. ""I think I got away with it:" Dumb thug is convicted after being caught bragging on Facebook even before jury began deliberations (Lol)." 6 June 2012. dailymail.co.uk. Daily Mail Feature Article. 11 June 2013.

Michael Shane Hagger

Police around the world have found that social media sites are powerful tools in catching criminals like Michael Shane Hagger, a shoplifter from New Zealand.

Hagger actually went to the Tauhara Paetiki Neighborhood Policing Team's Facebook page and dared the team to arrest him in June 2012. The genius actually taunted the police on Facebook.

The team had posted some information about Hagger on the page in the hope that somebody would turn him into the authorities. Hagger had earned the team's attention for not showing up in court to face petty theft charges. Instead, Hagger went to the page and insulted officers. He dared the cops to arrest him and responded to one of their posts with "hoo rah."

Worldwide Attention

If Hagger was on the run, he wasn't doing a very good job of it. His taunts were reported in the national media in New Zealand and then all over the world, including the United States. A fugitive is supposed to hide, not put his picture all over the place.

After a week of taunting various police departments in New Zealand on Facebook, Hagger eventually grew tired of life on the run. He left a post on another Facebook page that he would turn himself in at the local courthouse, which he did.

When he turned himself in, Hagger told reporters that he had underestimated the power of social media. In other words, he wasn't smart enough to realize that Facebook is a public medium and that anything he posted on it would be seen all over the world.

Taunting the police is bad enough, but doing it on their own Facebook page doesn't sound like a good way to keep out of jail. Fortunately for Hagger he didn't go to jail – his crimes were actually pretty minor.

Bibliography

Kirk, Stacy. "Facebook fugitive turns himself in." 7 July 2012. stuff.co.nz. Stuff News Article. 13 June 2013.

—. "Wanted man taunts police on Facebook." 5 July 2012. stuff.co.nz. Stuff News Article. 13 June 2013.

Michael Turley

YouTube, it seems, makes bragging about your crimes irresistible for some criminals. Case in point: Michael David Turley of Phoenix, Az. He not only committed a really dumb crime, he videotaped it and posted it on YouTube for everybody to see.

The crime was a brainless hoax that made absolutely no sense. Worse, he wanted to test police response to see how fast they would come. The reasons for the hoax are unknown but it is obvious how Turley and his accomplice got caught.

On July 28, 2012, Turley hired a 16-year old boy to dress up in a bed sheet and walk the streets of Phoenix carrying a fake rocket launcher. The boy was supposed to look like a terrorist in an attempt to scare the public. It was a miracle that the poor kid didn't get shot by police as he walked around a busy intersection.

Turley filmed the whole incident and posted it on YouTube. In an example of really bad taste, Turley titled his production: *Dark Knight Shooting Response, Rocket Launcher Police Test.* The "test" was conducted just eight days after a gunman killed 12 people at a screening of the Batman movie *The Dark Knight Returns* in Aurora, Colorado.

Insulting the Police on YouTube

In his voice-over commentary on the video, Turley even taunted police, saying it took them 15 minutes to respond to his provocation. So he not only posted evidence of the crime where it was easy to find, he also dared police to arrest him, and they did.

The stupidest thing about Turley's little movie was that there was apparently no motive for it. Turley gained absolutely nothing from the incident except an arrest on charges of "knowingly giving a false impression of a terrorist act," "child endangerment," and "contributing to the delinquency of a minor."

Turley's teenaged accomplice's name was not revealed because he was a minor. Police recommended that the hapless lad also face charges for a really dumb and completely senseless crime.

Bibliography

Cole, Chris. "Teen may also be charged in Phoenix "mock terrorist" case." 26 September 2012.

azcentral.com. Arizona Republic Newspaper Article.
7 June 2013.

Michael Anthony Fuller

Some crimes are just so incredibly dumb that it's hard to believe that criminals think that they can get away with them, but they do. A perfect example of this kind of excessive stupidity was North Carolina resident Michael Anthony Fuller.

Fuller tried to scam his local Wal-Mart out of nearly a million dollars in cash with a $1 million bill. There's one major problem with this strategy; there is no such thing as a $1 million bill in the United States and never has been. In fact, the largest bill currently in circulation in the United States is $100 according to the U.S. Treasury. The largest bill ever issued by the Treasury was the $100,000 bill, which hasn't been printed since 1935.

This didn't stop Fuller from walking into Wal-Mart putting $476 worth of merchandise into his cart, and going up to the register to pay. The genius expected that the cashier would give him nearly $1 million in cash as change. No store in the world, even Wal-Mart, keeps that amount of change around.

Using Play Money at the Checkout Line

Even though there is no such thing as a $1 million bill, Fuller kept insisting that it was real. He complained to the cashier and eventually to the manager. Eventually the staff got fed up with him and called the police.

Fuller's bill may not have been real, but the charges police slapped on him certainly were. He was booked for attempting to obtain property by false pretense (fraud) and using a forged instrument. The $17,500 bail Fuller had to pay was also real; hopefully he didn't try to use a $1 million bill to cover that as well.

The whole story is pathetic because $1 million bills are printed and sold in the United States as a novelty or a joke, meaning that Fuller tried to use play money to purchase real stuff at Wal-Mart. He might just go down as the world's dumbest criminal.

Bibliography

Matthews, Laura. "North Carolina Man Michael Anthony Fuller Tries to Use $1M Bill at Wal-Mart." 1 January 2012. ibtimes.com. International Business Times Feature Article. 13 June 2013.

U.S. Department of the Treasury "Denominations." n.d. treasury.gov. Denominations Frequently Asked Questions. 13 June 2013.

Michelle Hice

It doesn't take a criminal genius to steal large amounts of money, but it may take a genius to conceal the crime. At least that's what the case of

Michelle Hice, a terrible accountant and embezzler from Phoenix, demonstrates.

Hice got caught when the IRS audited a veterinary clinic where she was doing the books. The books showed that Hice had written checks totaling $130,000 to herself. That's right; she simply wrote checks to herself and made no attempt to cover up blatant theft.

If that wasn't bad enough, she simply deposited the money that she stole directly into her own bank account. When investigators from the Maricopa County Sheriff's Office looked into the case, they discovered that large amounts of money from a local church were also going into Hice's account. Hice had been hired to do the accounting for the church as well.

Leaving a Paper Trail

The bank statement revealed that Hice had deposited $25,000 in checks from the church in her account over a five-month period. She was supposed to be paid $300 a month for her "services." So she left paper and probably electronic records of her crime and lots of evidence for investigators to find.

Michelle Hice had actually expected that the IRS would not notice something like $130,000 missing from a business. She made no attempt to cover up the theft and then submitted the books to the Internal Revenue Service.

She didn't seem to realize that police would be able to subpoena her bank records and take a look at what was in her bank account. Obviously Hice isn't just a thief; she's a very bad accountant.

Nor does she learn from her mistakes; *The New Times* newspaper in Phoenix reported that Hice was on probation at the time she was arrested. She was on probation for embezzlement.

When she was arrested and booked for embezzlement, Hice gave police even more evidence to use against her. She was carrying a handgun, which is illegal for a convicted felon. Officers also found stolen property; namely two stolen credit cards in her possession. Some people it seems never learn from their mistakes.

Bibliography

Hendley, Matthew. "Michelle Hice, Apparently Terrible Accountant Accused of Cookin' the Books... Again." 21 February 2013. blogs.phoenixnetimes.com. News Blog Entry. 14 June 2013.

Middle School Terrorist

Stupid criminals often threaten or commit major crimes for the dumbest of reasons. A classic example of this was the unidentified 13-year-old in Nooksack Valley, Wash. who threated to blow up his middle school in order to get time to catch up on his homework.

The boy called 911 around 8 a.m. on Sept. 26, 2012 and said there was a bomb planted at Nooksack Valley Middle School. The idea behind the bomb threat was to get authorities to cancel school for the day. The boy wanted school cancelled because he hadn't completed his homework.

The lazy teenager hoped that he would be able to complete his homework and turn it in on time if he had an extra day off from school. The teenager was apparently more afraid of poor grades than the police.

Police responded to the threat by rerouting school buses to the local high school and having a bomb-sniffing dog search the middle school. The teachers and students in the middle school were evacuated from the building.

Officers eventually traced the bomb threat back to the boy's home. By the time they arrived there, the teen had left for school on the bus. Officers were waiting to arrest the boy when the bus arrived at school.

Class Was Never Cancelled

The teen was charged with a Class B felony for making a bomb threat and taken to juvenile detention. When he was arrested, the boy said he had made the threat because he was overwhelmed with schoolwork.

This teen has to be one of the dumbest criminals around because he didn't achieve his goal. Class was not canceled, so his homework was still late and he never had a chance to turn it in because he was in juvenile detention instead of class.

The identity of this teenaged genius was not revealed because laws in the U.S. make it illegal to reveal the identities of offenders under 18. That's probably a good thing because this young man probably doesn't want to be haunted by such a boneheaded stunt for the rest of his life.

Bibliography

Hutton, Caleb. "Student arrested for phony bomb threat at Nooksack School, says he needed to catch up on homework." 26 September 2012. bellinghmanherald.com. Bellingham Herald Newspaper Article. 8 June 2013.

Moses Wilson

There are some guys who just cannot resist a free beer, even if enjoying the suds might land them in jail. That's exactly what happened to Moses Wilson of Syracuse, N.Y. in February 2012.

Wilson's crime spree wasn't a very brilliant one – he first broke into an empty house, and since there was nothing else to steal there, he went into the basement to steal pipe, probably to sell for scrap metal. Some plumbing, especially the kind that is made from copper, can easily be sold for cash.

While he was in the house, Wilson found a case of beer in the basement. He opened the case and started drinking beers right then and there. After finishing off a few not-so-cold ones, Wilson finished stealing the pipes.

Okay, drinking beer out of a case that's been left sitting in a basement for a long time isn't a very bright idea. Leaving evidence that can lead the police to you and help prosecutors convict you is even dumber.

When the home's owner discovered that his house had been burglarized, he called the police. Police did a DNA test on the beer cans and identified Wilson, whose DNA is apparently on record with the police. His DNA was the only DNA on the empty beer cans he left in the house.

Had Wilson not drank the beer or simply taken it with him, he might have gotten away with the crime. Instead, he ended up in the county jail after police tracked him down and arrested him. The press reported he was facing charges of third degree burglary and petty larceny for his actions.

Successful criminals need to learn discipline and self-control if they don't want to get caught. The first step in such a regimen might be vowing never to eat or drink anything at the crime scene.

Bibliography

Patterson, Sara. "DNA on beer can left at scene of Syracuse crime helped authorities ID burglary suspect." 5 June 2013. syracuse.com. Syracuse Post-Standard Newspaper Article. 10 June 2013.

Nathan Teklemariam and Carson Rinehart

Almost everybody who owns a mobile phone has accidently dialed somebody on it at some time. This practice is sometimes called "butt dialing" because people leave phones turned on in their pockets and accidently sit on them. Two small time California hoodlums named Nathan Teklemariam and Carson Rinehart made the most embarrassing accidental call of all.

One of their phones accidently called 911 while they were planning to break into cars to get money to buy illegal drugs. The two morons were apparently sitting in their car in Fresno planning their latest criminal coup when they made the call.

To add insult to injury, they didn't realize what they had done. Instead, they went out and broke into a car with the police dispatcher listening. The dispatcher heard the two smash a car window with a hammer and yell that they had found prescription drugs.

Criminals Call 911 during Crime

Even though the fools were not paying attention, the 911 operator was. The alert dispatcher notified the police and a patrol car was dispatched to the area. Police quickly spotted the less than alert pair and pulled them over. Officers discovered stolen items and the tools for breaking into cars in their vehicle.

Interestingly enough, 911 operators were still listening when the police caught up with the pair. The two were wondering what they had done to attract police attention.

When you're planning a crime, you need to follow the advice that gets flashed on movie screens before the show starts: turn your phones off. You might not know who is listening. It might just be the police or emergency operators.

Bibliography

Burton, Connor. "Suspects Butt Dial 9-1-1 During Alleged Burglary ." 19 May 2013. abcnews.go.com. ABC News Article. 11 June 2013.

Nathaniel Troy Maye and Tiwanna Tenise Thomason

Even master criminals sometimes make really stupid moves that land them behind bars. Take super slick identity thieves Nathaniel Troy Maye and Tiwanna Tenise Thomason. The two were nabbed because they posted a picture of food on their Instagram website.

The "Bonnie and Clyde of Identity Theft" got themselves caught by posting a picture of their favorite meal, a Morton's steak and macaroni and cheese, on an Instagram "food porn" contest. They had enjoyed the meal on Jan. 7, 2013 with an undercover IRS agent.

The agent purchased a flash drive containing 50,000 stolen identities the two were peddling as part of a scheme to defraud the IRS. Troy Maye apparently enjoyed the meal that he ate during the meeting so much that he posted it online. The agent got the evidence against the two, but he was unable to identify or locate them.

Caught by Instagram

Another IRS agent eventually located a picture of the steak on Instagram and noted it had been posted on Jan. 7 and the poster was Troy Maye. Maye had used his own name as his screen name.

The super genius had committed an elementary error that even a novice hacker could use to track him down. Not only had the crook taken pictures of a major criminal transaction and shared them online, but the identity thief had also used his own identity, instead of one of the 700,000 fake IDs he allegedly had. Agents had no problem tracing him and arresting him.

A note to Mr. Maye: the next time you organize a major criminal conspiracy, consider using an alias.

116

It's not like you don't know where to get your hands on one.

The love of macaroni and cheese will cost Maye dearly – he's facing criminal charges that could land him in federal prison for up to 12 years.

Bibliography

Bluestone, Gabrielle. "Hipster Thieves Caught because they just had to Instagram their Food." 12 May 2013. gawker.com. Gawker News Feature. 11 June 2013.

McMahon, Paula. "Instagram 'food porn' photo leads IRS to identity thieves." 10 May 2013. articles.sunsentinel.com. Sun Sentinel Newspaper Article. 11 June 2013.

Velez, Adriana. "Stupid Criminal Caught Thanks to an Instagram Photo of Delicious Steak Dinner." 13 May 2013. thestir.cafemom.com/food. Blog Entry. 11 June 2013.

Paula Asher

Making stupid comments on Facebook isn't a crime, but that activity landed Paula Asher of Kentucky in jail. Asher ended up in the slammer after she used Facebook to try and rub some salt into the wounds of her victims.

Asher was arrested in July 2012 after slamming her car into a vehicle carrying four teenagers and driving off. The woman, who was apparently drunk at the time of the accident, was arrested shortly afterwards.

Judge Mary Jane Phelps was willing to let off Asher with a lighter sentence until some of her victims' parents showed the Judge a Facebook post that Asher had made.

Making Fun of the Victims on Facebook

Asher allegedly wrote: "My dumb ass got a DUI and I hit a car…LOL" LOL is an abbreviation for the term "laugh out loud." Asher went on social media and made fun of her victims for everybody to see.

The woman actually turned the court against her by laughing at her victims and making a mockery of the court. Worse, she did it in such a way that her victims' parents were sure to see and demand action.

Judge Phelps sent Asher to jail for 48 hours and had her charged with contempt of court. The Judge also ordered Asher to shut down her Facebook page.

The Judge was angry because she had been ordered to shut down her Facebook page earlier. Asher apparently didn't shut down the Facebook page and kept posting. She didn't think that somebody might check the page to see if it was still active.

Unlike some stupid criminals, Paula Asher apparently learned from her mistakes. She shut down her

Facebook page and has sworn off social media forever.

It is never a good idea to ignore a judge's directions. It's an even worse idea to leave an easily accessible record of the violation on Facebook for everybody to see.

Bibliography

Dolak, Kevin. "'LOL: Facebook Post after DUI Accident Lands Woman in Jail." 18 September 2012. abcnews.go.com. Feature Article. 7 June 2013.

Philadelphia Hair Salon Bandits

Armed robbery seems to attract the dumbest criminals around. A case in point is Philadelphia bandits Chau Tran, Tran Phoung, and Phuc Nguyen. The three gunmen actually robbed the wife of a local Mafia boss.

That's right, the three decided to target a mobster's wife as part of their robbery spree. On Dec. 21, 2010, the robbers entered a hair salon owned by Terri Staino in South Philadelphia. She opened the door thinking they wanted haircuts. Once in the salon, the three held up Mrs. Staino and took her wedding and engagement rings.

That was a really dumb move because Terri Staino is married to Anthony Staino, a known member of the Ligambi crime family and the reputed No. 2 man in the Philadelphia mob. It is a miracle the three lived to get arrested for what they had done.

Driving the Wrong Way on a One-Way Street

Fortunately for the bandits, they weren't on the street long enough for the Ligambi family to find them. Less than an hour after the robbery, police officers spotted them driving the wrong way on a one-way street. The officers pulled them over and found guns and the items stolen from Mrs. Staino in the car. They also discovered the loot from at least two other robberies in the vehicle.

The bandits were charged with robbery, criminal conspiracy, making terror threats, and other charges. They had better hope that there are no members or associates of the Ligambi family doing time at their prison.

Note to armed robbers everywhere – it pays to check out your targets before pulling a stickup. It's also a good idea to drive the right way on the streets because police tend to notice things like cars driving the wrong way.

Bibliography

Daily Mail Reporter "Dumb, dumber, dumberer: Three out of town thieves rob mafia boss's wife (then get caught driving wrong way down a one-way street)." 31 December 2010. dailymail.co.uk. Daily Mail Feature Article. 11 June 2013.

Robert Echeverria

Some criminals must like getting caught and going to jail. Otherwise, they wouldn't make it so easy for the police to find and arrest them. A few really considerate crooks, such as Robert Echeverria of Rialto, Calif., even provided officers with the evidence of their crimes to make convicting them easier.

Echeverria, a small time conman, was apparently concerned that the police were not paying enough attention to him. He rectified that by explaining one of his scams in a video and posting it on YouTube. Police saw the video and arrested Echeverria, who ended up spending 30 days in jail.

What's even dumber was the crime that Echeverria described in the video was called *How to Scam Del Taco*. Del Taco is a popular chain of fast food restaurants in California. In 2008, Echeverria figured out how to get food from the chain without paying.

He looked up the name of a company's CEO in the phone book. Then he called his local Del Taco and asked to speak to the manager. Echeverria claimed to be the CEO of an unidentified local company and said that Del Taco had messed up his order. Among other things, he threatened to call Del Taco's CEO and complain about the incident. He said he wouldn't complain if the manager filled the bogus order again.

The gullible manager fell for the scam and gave two accomplices Echeverria sent over the free food. The three would have gotten away with the questionable crime if they had not videotaped it and posted it on YouTube. Naming the video *How to Scam Del Taco* probably didn't help matters, either.

The video received around 40,000 hits, including at least one from the Rialto Police Department, which had an easy time identifying Echeverria. The video clearly shows his face. Echeverria was charged with burglary for the crime.

In addition to spending time in jail, Echeverria was also ordered to stay away from the Rialto Del Taco location. That meant he would have to start eating at Taco Bell. The moral of the story is if you want to be a successful con artist, don't reveal the details of your scams on YouTube.

Bibliography

Elsworth, Catherine. "Man who scammed free tacos, given jail term." 20 March 2008. telegraph.co.uk. Telegraph Newspaper Feature Article. 9 June 2013.

Ruth Amen

Criminals need to be careful in everything they do because one mistake can expose their wrongdoing. A criminal who was careless to the point of stupidity was Ruth Amen, an embezzler from Boca Grande, Fla.

Amen got caught because she threw her boss, whom she was stealing money from, an expensive surprise party. There was no way Ms. Amen could have paid for the party with her paltry salary, but she was able to pay for it with part of the $182,000 she stole from Gulf to Bay Realty.

As an office manager, Amen had access to the company's bank accounts. She had apparently been helping herself to company funds for years. The theft included $92,000 in unauthorized salary payments. Amen also took funds directly from the company's accounts. She also gave herself a $65,000 "raise" by not deducting insurance and other expenses from her paychecks.

Amen's boss got suspicious when she spent large amounts of the company's money on the party in early 2013 without permission. She showed all of her coworkers that she was spending company funds without authorization.

The suspicious boss decided to take a look at the books and found the stealing. The boss couldn't have been that bright because Amen had worked at the realty office for over 10 years, yet the thefts didn't come to light until the party.

Once the boss, who was not identified in news stories, was satisfied that embezzlement was taking place, he or she called in the Economic Crimes Unit of the Lee County Sheriff's Office. Sheriff's investigators checked out the allegations and found enough evidence to arrest Amen and book her for grand theft and scheming to defraud, which are legal terms for embezzlement.

If Amen hadn't thrown the party, she'd probably still be getting away with embezzlement. Instead, she was booked into the county jail and released on $150,000 bail. There's no word if she used the funds embezzled from the real estate office to cover her bail.

Bibliography

Gannett News Service "Woman Throws Boss Surprise Birthday Party, Gets Arrested for Embezzlement." 29 March 2013. digitriad.com. Wire Service News Article. 6 June 2013.

Moye, David. "Ruth Amen Arrested for Embezzling After Giving Boss a Surprise Birthday Party." 30 March 2013. huffingtonpost.com. Huffington Post News Article. 6 June 2013.

Pow, Helen. "Office manager of 10 years charged with embezzling $182,000 after surprise party she threw for boss on company dime sparked audit." 27 March 2013. dailymail.uk.co. Daily Mail News Article. 6 June 2013.

Ryan Letchford and Jeffrey Olson

The behavior of some dumb criminals is almost too incredible to believe. Take Ryan Letchford and Jeffrey Olson of Marlton, N.J. The two drunken numbskulls picked the worst possible vehicle of all to break into: a van belonging to the local police department. If that wasn't bad enough, the two men actually got themselves locked in the van.

What was possibly the stupidest crime in history began when the two were out drinking and partying in July 2011. The two spotted the van in Radnor, Pa. and decided to go inside and play with the equipment. The geniuses were actually playing with deadly weapons such as guns.

If that wasn't stupid enough, the drunks took pictures of themselves with police cameras so the cops would know exactly who had broken into the vehicle. To make matters even more pathetic, the two locked themselves in the van and called a friend for help.

Locked in the Paddy Wagon

The two locked themselves inside a metal cage in the back of the van when they pretended to be arrested. The cage is built to house criminals and it has an automatic locking mechanism that only police can open.

The friend called the police for help; the police came and let the two out then arrested them. The cop who was supposed to be in charge of the van, Constable Mike Connor, was apparently at home asleep when the van was broken into.

When Connor talked about the incident to the press, he called it unbelievable. Stupidity, it seems, knows no bounds, especially when it is combined with alcohol.

Letchford and Olson were booked for burglary and attempted vehicle theft for their actions. News articles didn't say if their unidentified buddy who had attempted to break into the vehicle would face charges too.

Bibliography

Daily Mail Reporter "It's the real-life Dumb and Dumber: Drunken men who broke INTO police arrested after they get locked inside." 21 July 2011. dailymail.co.uk. Daily Mail Feature Article. 11 June 2013.

WPVI TV "Police: NJ men locked selves in Pa. constable van." 18 July 2011. abclocal.go.com. News Article. 11 June 2013.

Ryan Homsley

What is it about Facebook that makes it such a siren song for idiotic criminals like Ryan Homsley? The Portland, Ore. resident actually told his Facebook friends that he had robbed a bank and even posted a link to a news story about the bank robbery on his Facebook page.

Homsley's short-lived career began in September 2010, when he walked into a bank in Tualatin, Ore., and told a teller he had a bomb. Homsley then took some cash and left a backpack and a box behind. When a bomb squad searched the packages, they discovered no explosives.

Homsley failed to disguise himself and let a surveillance camera get a good picture of him. The picture was published in the local press, which gave the robber the nickname the "Where's Waldo Bandit" because he had uncombed hair and glasses just like the title character in the popular children's books.

"I'm now a Bank Robber"

Almost as soon as he got home from robbing the Key Bank, Homsley began telling his Facebook friends about his new career. He posted links to news stories about the Where's Waldo Bandit and a video for a song called "Scooby Snacks" by the Fun Lovin' Criminals. The song was a about a bank robbery.

Homsley finally even told his friends: "I'm now a bank robber." A friend replied: "I am not surprised."

Facebook Friends from the FBI

Then to make sure people believed him, Homsley changed his Facebook profile picture to the surveillance camera photo from the bank robbery that had been published online. The photo attracted the attention of some new friends that Homsley probably didn't want. Two days after posting the picture, the friends—FBI agents—came to a hospital where Homsley was a patient and arrested him for bank robbery.

There are many things that should not be shared over social media. The fact that you've just committed a major felony is definitely one of them. There's no word on whether Homsley is telling his Facebook friends about his new life in federal prison.

Bibliography

Ross, Winston. ""The Where's Waldo Bank Robber" 28 September 2010. thedailybeast.com. Daily Beast Feature Article. 8 June 2013.

Stephfon Bennett

The old cliché is true; some criminals really do return to the scene of the crime. At least, gunman Stephfon

Bennett of Columbus, Ohio did. It's why Stephfon returned that made him one of the world's dumbest criminals.

Bennett was part of a trio of thugs that robbed and terrorized a couple in their home on Sept. 8, 2009. The crooks got away but Bennett was apparently smitten with the woman in the house - Diana Martinez.

He returned to the home a couple of hours later and asked her on a date. That's right, Bennett was dumb enough to think Diana would go out with him after he and his buddies had terrorized and robbed her. He also made the mistake of not thinking that she might call the police.

Robber asks Victim on Date

Perhaps Bennett considered himself to be such a master of disguise that Diana wouldn't recognize him.

She did and decided that she wanted nothing to do with him.

Martinez's cousin who was in the house called the police while Diana kept him busy. Police came right over and took Bennett on a different sort of date: to be booked into the local jail.

Returning to the crime scene and walking right up to the person you just robbed is dumb. Expecting that she might actually want to go on a date with you is even dumber.

Perhaps Stephfon Bennett should turn to online dating or singles bars next time he wants a hook up. Crime scenes are not a good place to go looking for love.

It's also interesting to note that Bennett asked Martinez if she had a boyfriend when he came back to ask her out. He already knew she had a boyfriend because he had robbed the man. If stupidity were measured in golden coins, Bennett would be doing

backstrokes in a Scrooge McDuck-sized silo of them
right now.

Bibliography

10TV.com. "Police: Robber Returned to Ask Victim
For Date." 8 September 2009. 10TV.com. News
Article 11 June 2013.

Suzanne Basham

There are some times when you should not call the police for help; for example, you should not call when you have just committed a crime. An example of this is Suzanne Basham of Springfield, Mo. She called police to report that the crack cocaine she had just bought was fake.

Basham, who is living proof that drugs do destroy your mind, had spent what she reported was $40 for crack from a local drug dealer. When the crack turned out to be nothing but sugar Basham called the police to file a complaint. This Einstein of crack addicts wanted to file a police complaint that her illegal drugs were fake.

The police did come to Basham's apartment, but she didn't get the justice she was expecting from them. Instead, the officers arrested her for possession of drug paraphernalia, namely a crack pipe. When the officers arrived, she asked them to go to the fraudulent drug dealers to get her money back.

The police did go to the drug house, but they had no evidence to search the place because the drugs were a fraud. Not only was Basham the only person arrested, but officers couldn't also even make a case against the fraudsters. It should be noted that the fraudsters may not have committed a crime, because all they sold was sugar. Selling sugar is not a crime, although they could be prosecuted for violating the sales tax laws.

Basham's brain was certainly addled by drugs if she actually expected police to get her money back from the crooks. Perhaps she didn't know that buying illegal drugs is illegal? Regardless, she thought it was a smart move to call the police and tell them that she had just broken the law. She also expected police to help her like a law-abiding citizen. It doesn't take years of law school to know that the police aren't going to assist you in committing a crime. The old service advertisement was right – drugs do destroy your brain.

Bibliography

Zennie, Michael. "Woman cited for drug possession after calling police to report dealer sold her sugar instead of crack cocaine." 14 January 2012. dailymail.co.uk. Daily Mail Newspaper Article. 13 June 2013.

The Dewsbury Six: The World's Dumbest Terrorists

Terrorists are nothing but criminals, and they can be just as dumb as any other criminals. The world's stupidest band of terrorists is probably the Dewsbury Six, a group of dimwitted Islamic militants from Birmingham, England.

The six wanted to spark religious war in England by staging an attack on a rally held by a rival terrorist group called the English Defense League, or EDL. The six got ready for the attack by putting knives and a homemade bomb in the trunk of a car. They then drove to Dewsbury, England, in April 2013 to blow up the members of the League.

There was only one problem; they arrived too late for the rally. When they reached the location for the attack, the event had ended and all of the EDL members had left. The terrorists actually arrived too late to commit their outrage. There was no one at the rally to kill, so the gang drove back home.

Caught by a Lack of Insurance

The six were eventually caught when their car was pulled over and impounded because one of them hadn't bought any insurance for it. The car didn't have insurance because the terrorist mastermind hadn't filled out the insurance application correctly. Police found bombs, knives, and documents declaring war on Queen Elizabeth in the vehicle's trunk.

A constable had pulled the men over in a routine traffic stop, but they appeared so harmless that the cops merely impounded the vehicle. Constables even dropped the fanatics off at the train station so they could get home.

Instead of starting a civil war between English racists and Islamic radicals, the six members of the terror cell ended up in jail. British newspaper accounts indicate that the six men—Omar Khan, Zohaib Kamran Ahmed, Mohammed Saud, Mohammed Hasseen, Anzal Hussain, and Jewel Udin—would receive long jail sentences.

To add insult to injury, press accounts indicate that police had been watching the terrorists for some time. Their brilliant moves included collecting money to finance their operation on the public street in full view of undercover police officers. The six also kept CDs of speeches of notorious terrorist preacher Anwar al-Awlaki in their car so police would be certain what they were dealing with.

The world would be a much safer place if all terrorists were as dumb as the Dewsbury Six.

Bibliography

Peachey, Paul. "Revealed: How plot to slaughter English Defense League Supporters failed as radical

144

Islamists' gang turned up late for rally." 30 April 2013. independent.couk. Independent Newspaper Article. 9 June 2013.

The Radnor Four

The world's four dumbest car thieves live in Radnor Township, Pa., near Philadelphia. The four broke into a towing company impound yard and stole a car impounded by police.

To make things really easy for police, the entire crime was captured by surveillance cameras. The cameras actually recorded Steve Rosso, David Kelly, Joseph Brennecke, and Timothy Spear breaking into the lot around 1 a.m. on April 16, 2013, then spending an hour moving vehicles around.

The four were trying to remove a 1999 Dodge Stratus that had been impounded for illegal parking. They apparently thought that they could avoid paying a $294 parking fine by taking the vehicle. One of them was also mad because he wouldn't be able to get the vehicle back until the next morning.

The geniuses apparently didn't realize that there was a record of the car's license plate number and registration at the impound yard. The record included the address of the vehicle's owner. All police had to do was go to his house and arrest him.

News articles didn't say which of the men the car belonged to, although it may not matter that much because the car was returned to the impound yard by police. The four thieves were jailed on a variety of charges, including burglary, theft, criminal trespass, and criminal mischief.

If the four had simply waited until the next morning and paid the fine, they could have gotten the car back without having to go to jail. Instead, they don't have the car or their freedom.

"This is probably Radnor's submission for world's dumbest criminals," Bill Colarulo, the police superintendent in the township, said.

The case wasn't a hard one for police to solve; Colarulo told a Philadelphia TV station that he solved the case over the phone. When he heard that a car had been stolen from the impound yard, the superintendent checked records and discovered who owned the vehicle. Some criminals make things way too easy for the police.

Bibliography

Bernstein, Jenn. "4 Men in Radnor Towing Lot Caught on Surveillance Video Taking Car." 1 May 2013. philadelphia.cbslocal.com. News Feature. 10 June 2013.

U.S. Chicken Machete Attackers

It's always a good idea to carefully pick a crime scene, especially in this age when surveillance cameras are everywhere. That's a lesson three knuckleheaded thugs from Patterson, N.J. learned the hard way.

Omar Villota, Tyree Seegers, and Johel Gomez savagely attacked another man with a machete and a pistol in a restaurant where cameras were clearly visible. The three nitwits committed dozens of felonies, and it was all caught on camera.

The attack occurred at a U.S. Chicken restaurant around 4 a.m. when the three walked in and attacked two other men. Seegers went after one man with a machete, and Villota pistol-whipped the second victim.

Criminals Hurt Each Other

The two were so incompetent that Seegers injured his cohort-in-crime with the machete. Seegers apparently hit Villota with such force that he almost chopped off his arm. That's right, he was so clumsy that he actually injured the man who was supposed to be helping him.

The only reason why the victim survived was that Seegers didn't know how to use the machete, Police Capt. Heriberto Rodriguez told the media. He actually brought a weapon he didn't know how to use to an assault.

Worst of all, the incompetent performance was caught on tape for everybody to see. Police then rubbed in the insult by posting the video on Facebook and releasing it to the media.

All three men were quickly identified and caught. Seegers was apparently so embarrassed by the incident that he went to the police station and turned himself in.

Obviously, criminals should never commit crimes, especially violent felonies in a public place where surveillance cameras are recording the action. It also helps to bring a weapon that you actually know how to use if you're planning to assault somebody, and it also pays to stand back when your buddy is slashing a victim with a machete.

Bibliography

CBS New York "Patterson Police Arrest 3 Men Caught on Tape in Machete Attack." 2 November 2011. newyork.cbslocal.com. News Article. 9 June 2013.

Victor Santos

Even some "brilliant" schemes can be very stupid, as the case of the late Victor Santos of Queens, N.Y. demonstrates. Santos got himself shot and killed when he tried to rob two undercover police detectives with an air pistol.

Santos was a habitual offender, with 39 arrests on his rap sheet, and obviously not a very bright man. Early in December, he decided to make some extra cash by robbing the crack dealers on the streets in the Ridgewood neighborhood of the New York City borough of Queens.

He went out around 10:45 p.m. and discovered what looked like a drug deal – two suspicious characters buying crack from a third suspicious character. The plan to rob drug-dealing gang members on their turf wasn't a very smart one to begin with.

"They're Cops You Idiot"

The whole scheme was dumber because Santos didn't even have a real gun. Instead, he had a Walther CP99 air pistol, which looks like a Glock 19, a popular semiautomatic pistol. The weapon he was carrying only shot compressed air; the weapons two of the suspicious characters were carrying were real guns that fired real bullets. The suspicious characters were undercover NYPD officers trying to make a drug bust.

To make matters worse, when Santos pulled the pistol, the drug dealer being arrested said, "They're cops, you idiot." Santos didn't listen and turned his "gun" on the cops.

The result was a very uneven gunfight in which Santos stood no chance. He was hit by five or six shots from the police guns. The dimwitted robber was taken to the Wyckoff Heights Medical Center, where he was pronounced dead on arrival.

Victor Santos' case shows that robbing drug dealers is a very stupid idea. Robbing undercover cops is an even stupider idea, and pointing a fake gun at police offers carrying real guns is probably the dumbest crime of all.

Bibliography

CBS New York "Police: Man Shot Dead by Officers Pulled Air Pistol That Looked Like Gun." 9 December 2012. newyork.cbslocal.com. News Article. 7 June 2013.

Vlado Taneksi

If there's an award for the world's dumbest murderer, it would have to go to the late Macedonian journalist and serial killer, Vlado Taneski. Taneski made one of the stupidest moves in the history of crime when he combined his day job as a newspaper reporter with his other activity of serial killing.

Taneski attracted a lot of attention with a series of articles for the newspaper in his hometown of Skopjie, Macedonia. The articles contained a vast amount of detail about a series of horrifying rapes and murders that were riveting the city. The problem was that they contained far too much detail.

Taneksi actually included details of the crimes that only the murderer and police investigators could have known in his stories. Detectives identified Taneksi as the murderer by reading the articles that he was writing.

The murders in question occurred between 2003 and 2008 and involved four older women, who were kidnapped and raped. Three of the bodies were dumped near Kicevo, a small town near Skopje, Macedonia's capitol. Macedonia is a small nation located just north of Greece.

Detectives were initially baffled by the case until they picked up a copy of the local daily newspaper, *The Nova Makedonija*. An article about the murder of Zivana Temelkkoska contained all sorts of details about the crime that detectives had declined to release to the press. Among the details were the method of murder—strangulation—and the signature weapon used by the killer—a piece of phone cord. Taneksi even outlined the time frame for the murders. He also noted that the victims had been bound with a piece of phone cord.

After reading Taneski's article on May 19, 2008, and seeing his scoop, police went straight to the newspaper office and arrested the mild-mannered reporter and father of two.

Taneksi will never collect the award for stupidest serial killer because he died under suspicious circumstances at a local prison. He drowned in a toilet bowl in what police described as a "suicide." Obviously, journalists should never write in detail about their own crimes.

Bibliography

Smith, Helena. "The shocking story of the newspaper crime reporter who knew too much." 23 June 2008. guardian.co.uk. Guardian Feature Article. 6 June 2013.

CPSIA information can be obtained
at www.ICGtesting.com
Printed in the USA
FSHW012124141118
53808FS